# Recipes for
# *Warming Hearts*

### *It's the little things!*

Making a difference in the lives of those near and dear to us can be such a simple thing! Baking up some warm muffins to greet your family, treating the neighborhood pets to some doggone delicious treats or surprising a good friend with a new recipe to try are all small gestures sure to brighten someone's day.

In this little book, you'll find many more genuine ideas like these for letting others know just how much they're loved and appreciated... whether they are generous volunteers, helpful neighbors, dear friends or beloved family members.

We've also gathered a sampling of stories from our Gooseberry Patch family to warm your heart, along with a collection of our best-loved recipes for heartfelt gifts from the kitchen and our favorite ideas for sharing the love all year 'round.

No matter whose heart you're warming, we hope these pages will inspire you to spread some kindness today!

One of the most heartwarming events in my life was the day we brought our daughter Sydney home. My husband and I had already raised three boys…a full house by most people's standards! But big families seemed natural to us. My husband is the oldest of ten kids and I was one of six, so we were used to the busy commotion of a full house.

Instead of adding to our family in the "traditional" way, we wanted to help a less fortunate child in the world. Since we both love travel, and had been to Russia before, we decided to go there to adopt. After seemingly never-ending paperwork and background checks, in late 1996 we were finally ready to take the thirteen-hour flight to Russia to pick up our little Sydney.

When we arrived at the orphanage, all the kids ran or crawled over to us in hopes of being chosen. It was heart-breaking…but we were happy to leave donations of clothing, food and medical supplies to help improve their lives in some small way.

Sydney was frail and malnourished and unable to crawl, let alone walk. But she was as sweet and happy as can be. She immediately bonded with us.

We flew home a few days later. Unbeknownst to us, my entire family was waiting in Ohio to welcome Sydney into the family. Since they all lived out of state, it was a huge gesture on their part, and one that I will never forget.

My birthday happened to fall on Thanksgiving that year, so three days after returning home, we celebrated my birthday, Thanksgiving and Sydney's arrival. Later that day, I laid my daughter down for her nap and crawled in bed beside her…totally exhausted but so happy to have my family complete!

—Jo Ann

Love is,
above all else,
*the gift of
oneself.*

—Jean Anouilh

Thanks

# Send a Heartfelt Message ♥ of Thanks

Show your appreciation for all the people in our lives who generously give their time all year long. Whether they're serving our communities or our country, they all make our lives a little bit better.

## Community leaders...

- [ ] active-duty military
- [ ] community advocates
- [ ] firefighters
- [ ] foster parents
- [ ] literacy volunteers
- [ ] local government leaders and volunteers
- [ ] mentors
- [ ] nurses
- [ ] parent classroom volunteers
- [ ] police officers
- [ ] postal carriers
- [ ] PTO volunteers
- [ ] Scout leaders and volunteers
- [ ] Sunday School teachers
- [ ] teachers
- [ ] youth sports coaches
- [ ] veterans

In late summer, divide some favorite perennial flowers and share them with a dear friend...the beginning of a delightful friendship garden.

When you're shopping for back-to-school supplies, pick up a few extra packages of crayons or notepaper for your child's teacher...or ask what supplies they need most, and surprise them with a donation.

Time for a spring cleaning? Gather outgrown coats, unused cell phones, sports equipment, toys, books and more. There are many organizations that will be glad to receive your extra items!

Cook a meal for someone...whether it's a new parent or someone who's new to the neighborhood, homemade goodness is sure to be appreciated!

Taking a trip? Pick up the extra little shampoo bottles from your hotel room. Individual-size toiletries and free samples are just the right size to donate to a local shelter.

Are your kids growing up before your eyes? Donate their gently used things to a local children's charity. Many need school supplies, shoes, clothes and even toys and books!

Missing a far-away friend? Pack up a care package full of homebaked treats and other hometown mementos. Just right for a new college student, a friend who's moved to a new city or a soldier serving overseas.

Special Delivery

## ...and everyday helpers!

- [ ] babysitters
- [ ] bus drivers
- [ ] childcare providers
- [ ] co-workers
- [ ] dog walkers and groomers
- [ ] friends & family
- [ ] furry pals
- [ ] grandparents
- [ ] hair stylists
- [ ] home cleaners
- [ ] home health aides
- [ ] neighbors
- [ ] pet sitters
- [ ] _____
- [ ] _____
- [ ] _____
- [ ] _____

*♥ Warm your family's hearts by turning an ordinary day into a special occasion! Gather the family around the table and enjoy these classic comfort-food dishes.*

## French Toast Berry Bake

*A year-round treat…pile on fresh berries in the summer!*

12 slices French bread, sliced
    1-inch thick
5 eggs, beaten
2-1/2 c. milk
1-3/4 c. brown sugar, packed and
    divided
1-1/2 t. vanilla extract
1-1/4 t. cinnamon

Optional: 1/2 t. nutmeg, 1/4 t.
    ground cloves
Optional: 1 c. chopped pecans
1/2 c. butter, melted
2 c. blueberries, strawberries,
    raspberries and/or
    blackberries

Arrange bread slices in a greased 13"x9" baking pan; set aside. In a bowl, combine eggs, milk, one cup brown sugar, vanilla, cinnamon and desired spices. Whisk until blended; pour over bread. Cover and refrigerate for 8 hours to overnight. Let stand at room temperature 30 minutes before baking. Sprinkle with pecans, if using. Combine melted butter and remaining brown sugar; drizzle over top. Bake, uncovered, at 400 degrees for 30 minutes. Sprinkle with berries and bake an additional 10 minutes, or until a fork comes out clean. Serves 12.

# Monkey Bread

*Kids love this yummy, pull-apart bread with the funny name!*

1/2 c. butter
1 c. brown sugar, packed
3 T. cinnamon, divided

1/2 c. sugar
2 12-oz. tubes refrigerated
    biscuits, cut in quarters

Melt butter, brown sugar and one tablespoon cinnamon in a small saucepan. Heat until bubbly; set aside. Blend remaining cinnamon and sugar in a small bowl. Roll biscuits in cinnamon-sugar mixture; arrange in a greased Bundt® pan. Pour brown sugar mixture over top; bake at 325 degrees for 30 minutes or until golden. Let stand several minutes before turning out of pan. Serve warm. Makes 10 to 12 servings.

*Baking together is such a fun family activity! As you measure, mix and bake together, you're creating memories as well as sweet treats.*

# Garlicky Herbed Pork Roast

*Your family will ooh and aah over this gorgeous roast!*

4 to 5-lb. pork roast
4 cloves garlic, slivered
1 t. dried thyme
1/2 t. dried sage
1/2 t. ground cloves

1 t. salt
1 t. lemon zest
Optional: 2 T. cold water,
      2 T. cornstarch

Cut 16 small pockets into roast with a knife tip; insert garlic slivers. Combine thyme, sage, cloves, salt and zest; rub over roast. Place roast in a slow cooker. Cover and cook on low setting for 7 to 9 hours, or on high setting for 4 to 5 hours. Allow roast to stand 10 to 15 minutes before slicing. Remove and discard garlic pieces. If thicker gravy is desired, strain juices into a saucepan over medium heat; bring to a boil. Mix together water and cornstarch until dissolved; gradually add to saucepan. Cook until thickened, about 5 minutes. Serve gravy over sliced pork. Serves 8 to 10.

*Stay in for a cozy night with the family...fill the table with lots of tasty snacks and pull out a board game or two.*

# Old-Fashioned Chicken Pot Pies

*Invite the whole family over for this crowd-pleasing dish!*

4 frozen pie crusts, thawed and
    divided
5 to 6 boneless, skinless chicken
    breasts, cooked and chopped
1 onion, chopped
10-3/4 oz. can cream of chicken
    soup

10-3/4 oz. can cream of potato
    soup
2  15-oz. cans mixed vegatables,
    drained
8-oz. container sour cream
salt and pepper to taste

Line two 9" pie plates with one crust each; set aside. Combine remaining ingredients except crusts in a large bowl; mix well. Divide between pie plates; top with remaining crusts. Crimp crusts to seal; cut several slits in top crusts. Bake at 350 degrees for 35 to 45 minutes, until bubbly and crusts are golden. Makes 2 pies, 6 servings each.

As the sun sets around dinnertime, light a candle or two at the family table. It'll make an ordinary meal seem special!

# Banana Split Bars

*A delicious new way to enjoy a classic treat!*

1/3 c. butter, softened
1 c. sugar
1 egg, beaten
1 banana, mashed
1 t. vanilla extract
1-1/4 c. all-purpose flour
1 t. baking powder

1/4 t. salt
1/3 c. chopped walnuts
2 c. mini marshmallows
1 c. semi-sweet chocolate chips
1/3 c. maraschino cherries,
    quartered

Stir butter and sugar together; add egg, banana and vanilla. Stir in flour, baking powder and salt; add nuts. Pour into a greased 13"x9" baking pan; bake at 350 degrees for 20 minutes. Remove from oven; sprinkle with marshmallows, chocolate chips and cherries. Bake for an additional 10 to 15 minutes; cool. Cut into bars. Makes about 2 dozen.

Dress up these easy, pleasing bars! Instead of cutting them into bars or squares, cut diagonally across the dish for pretty little diamonds or use mini cookie cutters for special occasions.

# Super-Easy Puddin' Cake

*A topping of fresh berries turns this simple cake into an elegant treat!*

18-1/4 oz. pkg. devil's food cake
    mix
2  3.4-oz. pkgs. instant
    chocolate pudding mix

2 c. raspberries
Optional: whipped topping

Prepare cake mix according to package directions. Bake in 2 greased 9"
round cake pans; cool. Prepare pudding mixes according to package
directions. Place one cake layer on a cake plate; top with half the
pudding. Place the other layer on top; cover with remaining pudding.
Sprinkle berries and whipped topping, if using, on top of cake. Makes
8 servings.

Need a cake stand in
a jiffy for your special
creation? Simply turn
a bowl over and set a
pretty plate on top.

13

My dad has been a small-town mailman for over twenty years now but I remember how hard the job was for him at first. The long hours, dozens of miles walked every day and the weather all presented challenges. They can still be tough, especially in snowy Ohio winters!

I never heard him complain though…and what I remember most are the stories of his customers. In addition to remembering the names and faces of folks on his route, he always made sure to learn the names of the kids and dogs too.

Handing out candy canes when delivering holiday cards and carrying dog biscuits in his pocket year 'round have made him a beloved part of the neighborhoods he's served. I'm sure it's these kinds of connections that have given him the most satisfaction through the years.

Each year, around Christmas and his birthday, he brings home all sorts of homemade goodies from these folks…cookies, fudge, breads, even whole pies! His customers never miss a chance to show their appreciation for mail delivered with a smile.

—Jen at Gooseberry Patch

'Tis the *sweet,*
*simple things*
of life which are the
real ones after all.

—*Laura Ingalls Wilder*

*Spread the cheer by sharing these dishes with neighbors, friends and co-workers...each is not only delicious but perfectly portable, too!*

## Apple Scones
*So yummy served warm from the oven!*

2 c. all-purpose flour
1 t. baking powder
1 t. salt
3 T. butter
1/4 c. sugar

1 c. apple, peeled, cored and
    minced
1 egg, beaten
2/3 c. milk
Garnish: 2 T. butter, 2 T. sugar

Combine flour, baking powder and salt in a mixing bowl. Cut in butter with a pastry blender until mixture resembles coarse crumbs. Add sugar and apple. Mix in egg and milk; stir until a soft dough forms. Knead until well blended. Spread in a greased 12"x8" baking pan. Bake at 450 degrees for 25 minutes. Cut into 2"x2" squares; cut each square in half diagonally. Spread tops with butter; sprinkle generously with sugar. Serve warm. Makes 4 dozen.

*Surprise a friend with a "Tea for Two" party! Wrap up these scones in a new tea towel, and tuck in several of her favorite teas.*

# Chocolate & Peanut Butter Popcorn

*A yummy pick-me-up for a good friend…deliver with a new book or magazine for an extra-special treat!*

14 c. popped popcorn
3 c. crispy rice cereal
2 c. dry-roasted peanuts

1-1/2 lbs. melting chocolate, chopped
3 T. creamy peanut butter

In a very large bowl, mix popcorn, cereal and peanuts; set aside. Combine chocolate and peanut butter in a microwave-safe bowl. Microwave on high for 2 to 3 minutes until melted, stirring after every minute. Pour over popcorn mixture, tossing to coat well. Spread onto a large greased non-stick baking sheet; cool completely. Break apart; store in an airtight container up to 5 days. Makes about 20 to 22 cups.

*A delightful way to deliver Chocolate & Peanut Butter popcorn…cut a "window" from a lunch bag using a cookie cutter as the stencil. Glue a square of cellophane inside the bag over the cut-out, then place a plastic zipping bag filled with popcorn inside!*

# Creamy White Chicken Chili

*A quick & easy favorite that's sure to please!*

6  15-1/2 oz. cans Great
   Northern beans, drained and
   rinsed
3  5-oz. cans chicken, drained
6  c. chicken broth
3  c. shredded Monterey Jack
   cheese
2  4-oz. cans diced green chiles

12-oz. container sour cream
1 T. olive oil
2 t. ground cumin
1 t. garlic powder
1-1/2 t. dried oregano
1/4 t. white pepper
Optional: 2 onions, chopped

Combine all ingredients in a large stockpot. Simmer for 20 minutes until heated through. Serves 16 to 20.

Transporting a full pot
of soup can be tricky,
so here's a handy tip.
Slip a large rubber band
under one handle, twist
it around the knob on the
lid and wrap under the
other handle. The lid will
stay secure!

# Mini Sausage Muffins

*These savory little bites are perfect served alongside soups and salads!*

1 lb. ground pork sausage,
   browned and drained
10-3/4 oz. can Cheddar cheese
   soup

1/2 c. plus 2 T. water
3 c. biscuit baking mix

Mix all ingredients well. Fill lightly-greased mini muffin cups 2/3 full.
Bake at 350 degrees for 10 to 12 minutes, or until golden. Makes about 4
dozen.

Welcome newcomers to the neighborhood by hand-delivering a
basket of breakfast goodies! Tuck in a list of your suggestions for
the best local destinations too.

# Muffin Pan Rolls

*A warm basket of bread is always welcome! Pair with a homemade butter blend for a gift that's sure to be remembered.*

1 pkg. active dry yeast
3/4 c. warm water
2 c. all-purpose flour, sifted and
    divided
3/4 t. salt

1-1/2 T. sugar
1 egg, beaten
2 T. shortening, melted and
    slightly cooled

Dissolve yeast in warm water; let stand 3 minutes. Add one cup flour, salt, sugar, egg and shortening. Beat until smooth. Add remaining flour and stir until flour is fully blended in. Let dough rise until double in size, about 30 minutes. Divide dough by 12; roll into balls and place in a lightly greased muffin pan. Let rise again for 30 minutes. Bake at 425 degrees for 15 minutes. Makes 12.

Invite family & friends
to share tried &
true favorite dishes
and create a recipe
scrapbook...
a great gift for a
new cook in
the family.

# Honey Butter

3/4 c. butter, softened
3/4 c. honey

3/4 c. powdered sugar
1 t. cinnamon

Blend together all ingredients; store in an airtight container and refrigerate. Use within 2 weeks. Makes about 2 cups.

# Fresh Herb Butter

1/2 c. butter, softened
1/4 c. fresh herbs, chopped, such
as basil, thyme, sage, parsley,
dill, chives, tarragon, oregano,
marjoram or rosemary

1 t. sea salt
1 t. pepper

Blend all ingredients together. Spoon onto a sheet of wax paper and shape into a log. Twist ends of wax paper to seal. Refrigerate one hour to allow flavors to blend. Use within 2 weeks. Makes 1/2 cup.

Whether sweet or savory, a
new butter blend is an
oh-so-yummy way to jazz up
a simple loaf of bread!

# Molasses Oat Cookies
*Old-fashioned goodness…just like Grandma used to make!*

1/2 c. shortening
2 eggs
1-1/4 c. sugar
1/2 c. molasses
1-3/4 c. all-purpose flour
1 t. baking soda
1 t. salt

2 t. cinnamon
2 c. quick-cooking oats,
   uncooked
1 c. golden raisins
Optional: 1/2 c. chopped nuts

Combine shortening, eggs, sugar and molasses in a medium bowl; mix thoroughly. Stir in flour, baking soda, salt and cinnamon. Add oats, raisins and nuts, if using; mix well. Drop by teaspoonfuls onto lightly greased baking sheets. Bake at 400 degrees for 8 to 10 minutes. Makes 3 to 4 dozen.

Drop cookies travel best…
be sure to double-wrap the
batch in aluminum foil
and pack closely together
to minimize shifting.

# Spiced Pumpkin Bars

*What a delightful way to celebrate the flavors of fall any time of year!*

3 eggs, beaten
15-oz. can pumpkin
1 c. sugar
12-oz. can evaporated milk
1 t. vanilla extract
1 t. cinnamon
1/2 t. ground ginger

1/4 t. ground cloves
18-1/4 oz. pkg. spice cake mix
3/4 c. butter, thinly sliced
1 c. chopped pecans
Optional: 16-oz. can cream
    cheese frosting

In a large bowl, beat eggs and pumpkin together. Blend in sugar, evaporated milk, vanilla and spices. Pour into a greased 13"x9" baking pan. Sprinkle dry cake mix evenly over top of batter. Dot with butter slices, making sure to place some in corners of pan. Sprinkle pecans over top. Bake at 350 degrees for 55 minutes. Cool; frost, if desired, and cut into bars. Makes 12 to 16 servings.

*Dip a mini cookie cutter in cinnamon and lightly press into the frosting on each bar... such a pretty touch!*

*Although it seems like only yesterday that I graduated from high school, let's just say it's been a few years. My high school girlfriends were simply the best, and I thought we'd never lose touch. But life is funny that way…you grow up, settle down and start a family. Suddenly, life gets so busy and friendships fall by the wayside.*

*Then, one day, your kids are grown and you realize just how important it is to reconnect with all those people you care about. For me, it happened about five years ago. I ran into a girlfriend while shopping and as we were chatting, we just clicked. It was like no time had passed! Right then, we decided to get all the girls together and do something fun.*

*I'd always heard that everlasting friends can go long periods of time without speaking and never question the friendship, but it was that first get-together with the girls that made me believe it. It didn't matter how long it had been or how far we'd lived from each other. We picked right up where we left off!*

*Since that first time, we've continued to get together a few times a year. Sometimes we plan a craft party, white elephant gift exchange or a plant swap. Other times, we've been known to just sit around the fire and sip wine and tell stories in my little log cabin.*

*But one thing never changes…the good food and great friends. It's a "recipe" that always warms my heart.*

*—Vickie*

Have friends,
not for the
sake of receiving,
*but of giving.*

—*Joseph Roux*

# Wrap It Up!

**Make your heartfelt gifts really shine with these clever packaging ideas.**

For a quick & easy airtight goodie bag, cut some colorful paper the same width as a plastic zipping bag, fold in half and decorate. Attach with double-sided tape or staples and it's ready to give.

Next time you're giving a gift from the kitchen, decorate a lunch bag with stencils or cheerful rubber stamps. Fill with treats, fold the top over and punch two holes in the top. Slide a candy stick or a long-stemmed flower through the holes for a sweet gift bag!

Giving tickets to an event or concert? Showcase them in a vintage photo frame...a keepsake they'll always treasure.

Have a favorite gardener on your list? Tuck a new pair of gloves and a few packets of seeds inside a new terra-cotta pot. Simply turn the saucer upside down and place over the opening of the pot, and secure the "lid" with a plump bow.

Package a gift of cookies in a jiffy! Decorate a cardboard mailing tube with stickers or cut-outs and slide in a plastic-wrapped stack of cookies.

Giving a cookbook or another gift they'll use in the kitchen? Wrap it up in a new apron or tea towel, and the wrapping becomes a lasting gift too.

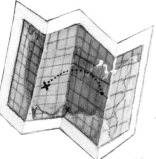

Look for whimsical giftwrap in unexpected places! Road maps and brown kraft paper are wonderful for wrapping oversized presents, while sheets of scrapbooking and origami paper are just the right size for smaller gifts.

Look to nature for clever package toppers: holly leaves and evergreen in the winter, twigs and tropical leaves in the summer, and fall leaves in the autumn.

*These dishes are not only delicious, but can be frozen and enjoyed later...perfect for new parents, college students or anyone who's feeling a little short on time!*

## Tuscan Soup

*Savory and filling...a perfect warm-you-up meal!*

1 lb. ground pork sausage
3/4 c. onion, diced
1 slice bacon, diced
1-1/4 t. garlic, minced
2 T. chicken bouillon granules
4 c. water

2 potatoes, halved lengthwise and
    cut into 1/4-inch strips
2 c. kale, thinly sliced
3/4 c. whipping cream

Brown sausage in a large pot over medium heat; drain and set aside. Add onion and bacon to pot; cook over medium heat until onion is almost translucent. Add garlic; cook for one minute. Add bouillon, water and potatoes; simmer for 15 minutes, until potatoes are tender. Stir in kale, sausage and whipping cream; heat through over low heat without boiling. Serves 6 to 8.

When freezing soup, be sure to leave a little headspace at the top...it needs room to expand as it freezes.

# Glazed Lemon Bread

*Serve one loaf to your family for breakfast...deliver the second loaf to a friend!*

| | |
|---|---|
| 3/4 c. shortening | 1/4 t. baking soda |
| 1-1/2 c. sugar | 1/4 t. salt |
| 3 eggs | 3/4 c. buttermilk |
| 2-1/4 c. all-purpose flour | zest of one lemon |

Thoroughly combine shortening and sugar; add eggs one at a time, beating well after each addition. In a separate mixing bowl, combine flour, baking soda and salt; add to sugar mixture. Stir in buttermilk and zest. Divide into 2 greased 9"x5" loaf pans; bake at 350 degrees for 30 to 35 minutes. Pour the Glaze over the tops while still warm. Makes 2 loaves.

## Glaze:

| | |
|---|---|
| 3/4 c. powdered sugar | Optional: 1 to 2 t. water |
| juice of one lemon | |

Stir together sugar and lemon juice until smooth; add water if needed to achieve desired consistency.

*Make sure your bread stays fresh and tasty...let the loaf cool completely before wrapping well in plastic wrap or aluminum foil.*

# Chicken Tetrazzini

*An easy-to-reheat meal sure to be appreciated by new parents!*

1/2 c. butter
1/2 c. all-purpose flour
1/2 t. salt
1/4 t. pepper
2 c. chicken broth
2 T. sherry or chicken broth
2 c. milk or whipping cream

8-oz. pkg. spaghetti, cooked
2 c. cooked chicken, cubed
3/4 c. grated Parmesan cheese,
   divided
Optional: 4-oz. can sliced
   mushrooms, drained

Melt butter in a large saucepan over medium heat. Add flour, salt and pepper; cook until bubbly. Add broth, sherry or broth and milk or cream; bring to a boil for one minute. Stir in spaghetti, chicken, 1/4 cup Parmesan cheese and mushrooms, if using; mix well. Spread in a lightly greased 13"x9" baking pan; sprinkle with remaining Parmesan cheese. Bake, uncovered, at 350 degrees for 30 minutes. Makes 6 to 8 servings.

*Sharing a casserole? Be sure to tie on a tag with the recipe. A hand-written recipe will be treasured long after the food disappears.*

Chicken Tetrazzini
1/2 c. butter
1/2 c. all-purpose flour
1/2 t. salt
1/4 t. pepper
2 c. chicken broth

# Beefy Porcupine Meatballs

*The rice makes these meatballs look like spiky porcupines...kids and adults alike will enjoy these savory treats!*

8-oz. pkg. beef-flavored rice
   vermicelli mix, divided
1 lb. ground beef

1 egg, beaten
2-1/2 c. water
cooked egg noodles

Combine rice vermicelli mix with ground beef and egg, setting aside seasoning packet from mix. Shape into small meatballs; brown on all sides in a skillet. Drain. Combine contents of seasoning packet with water; pour over meatballs. Cover and simmer over low heat for 30 minutes. Serve meatballs and sauce over cooked egg noodles. Serves 4 to 6.

Is your garden rewarding you with a bounty of blooms? Share the wealth by leaving a cheery bouquet on a neighbor's door...an unexpected delight!

# Cream Cheese-Filled Cupcakes

*No need to frost these sweet cakes, so they're super easy to pack and deliver!*

18-1/4 oz. pkg. German
   chocolate cake mix
1 c. mini semi-sweet chocolate
   chips

1/3 c. sugar
1 egg, beaten
8-oz. pkg. cream cheese, softened

Prepare cake mix according to package directions. Fill paper-lined muffin cups 1/2 full. Combine remaining ingredients; drop by teaspoonfuls onto batter. Bake at 350 degrees for 20 to 25 minutes. Cool completely. Makes about 2 dozen.

A friend who bakes would love to find a mini-cookbook slipped in the pocket of a cheery new potholder. Don't forget to tuck in recipe cards sharing some of your family's favorites too.

# Cheddar Crackers

*Crispy and zesty…the perfect partner for a warming bowl of soup!*

2 c. shredded sharp Cheddar
  cheese
1/2 c. butter, softened

1-1/2 c. all-purpose flour
1/2 t. garlic salt
1/4 t. cayenne pepper

Combine cheese and butter in a large mixing bowl; blend with an electric mixer until well mixed. Add remaining ingredients; mix well. Divide dough in half; shape each into a 7-inch long roll. Wrap in plastic wrap; refrigerate for at least one hour. Slice into 1/4-inch thick rounds; arrange on an ungreased baking sheet. Bake at 350 degrees for 15 minutes; cool on a wire rack. Store in an airtight container in the refrigerator for up to one week or freeze up to 3 months. Makes about 4-1/2 dozen.

Pack up a batch of savory
Cheddar Crackers along
with a favorite soup mix in
a ceramic soup bowl…great
for a loved one feeling
under the weather!

Made with LOVE

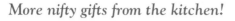

# Coconut Brownies in a Jar

*A thoughtful gift that can be enjoyed now or later.*

1/3 c. chopped walnuts
1/2 c. semi-sweet chocolate chips
1/3 c. sweetened flaked coconut
2/3 c. brown sugar, packed

3/4 c. sugar
1/3 c. baking cocoa
1-1/2 c. all-purpose flour

Layer ingredients in the order listed in a wide-mouth, one-quart canning jar. Pack each layer down as tightly as possible before adding the next layer. Seal tightly; attach instructions (on the next page).

It's easy to create a custom jar to hold mixes. Use etching cream to paint initials on a clear glass jar, or brush etching cream over a rubber stamp to stamp on whimsical designs.

# Coconut Brownies
## in a Jar

### Instructions:

Place mix in a large bowl. Add 2 beaten eggs, 2/3 cup oil and one teaspoon vanilla extract. Blend well. Spread in a greased 8"x8" baking pan. Bake at 350 degrees for 30 minutes, or until center tests done. Makes one dozen brownies.

Enjoy!

Don't forget to include the baking instructions! Copy the above label and attach it to the jar.

# Gentle Oatmeal Body Scrub

*This simple mix will leave skin glowing!*

1 c. quick-cooking oats,
    uncooked
24 drops of essential oils, in
    desired combination, such as
    orange, lavender, rosewood
    and chamomile

Optional: 1 T. dried lavender
    petals

Process oats in a food processor until very fine. In a bowl, mix oats with dried lavender, if using; add essential oils drop by drop, stirring constantly to avoid clumps. Store in an airtight jar; use within 6 months.

## Instructions:

Mix one to 2 tablespoons of Gentle Oatmeal Body Scrub with enough water to form a paste. Apply to wet skin in a circular motion. Rinse well with warm water and pat dry.

*Tie on a new bath poof for a perfect pampering gift!*

# Pepperminty Lip Balm

*So cool and refreshing, everyone on your list will want some!*

6 T. almond oil
2 t. honey
4 t. beeswax, grated

5 drops vitamin E oil
5 drops peppermint essential oil
8 1/2-oz. lidded pots

In a double boiler, melt almond oil, honey and beeswax together. Remove from heat, allowing mixture to cool slightly. Add vitamin E and peppermint oils; stir until well blended. Spoon into pots and allow to cool before covering. Makes 8 pots.

Gather your pals together for a girls' night in and mix up a batch of Pepperminty Lip Balm...a sure-fire way to lift spirits!

# Wipe-Off Memo Board

*Makes a great gift…use vinyl lettering to add a monogram or a favorite quote to personalize!*

picture frame with glass front
patterned scrapbook paper, large
    enough to fit frame
dry-erase marker

Optional: vinyl cut letters to
    personalize
Optional: four heavy-duty
    magnets, hot glue gun

Trim paper to fit frame. Use vinyl letters to personalize, if desired. Place paper in frame. To use, stand memo board on an easel, or attach four magnets with a hot-glue gun and hang on the refrigerator. Write on glass front with dry-erase maker; wipe off with a soft cloth.

Simply change the
background paper for
a different look all
throughout the year. A
treasured piece of vintage
fabric would be pretty too!

# Love You!

- Plant flowers
- Mail Gift
- Bake Cookies
- Trip to Zoo
- Tea with Granny

Dry-Erase

Spread the love...share an encouraging word, a heartfelt compliment or kind smile each and every day!

We weren't in the market for a dog when Scruffy appeared in our lives. It had been more than five years since we had to say goodbye to our old dog, and although my kids asked repeatedly for a pet (a dog, a cat, an anything!), I always changed the subject. I just couldn't face another emotional good-bye.

Then, during one of the harshest winters we've had in years, my mom found a stray dog wandering in the snow. When I first laid eyes on the beleaguered pooch, it was clear that he had been on his own for a very long time. His long coat was matted from the tip of his tail to the tops of his ears. He was underweight, and once we painstakingly cut off all fur mats, he was nothing but skin and bones. He was also pretty darn cute with his big dark brown eyes and tiny black nose, and his streak of bad luck hadn't broken his spirit.

My no-dog resolve was sorely tested. Mom said she'd keep the dog while we decided. Perhaps knowing that his fate was in the balance, the little dog was a perfect houseguest…and my kids, knowing that their futures as pet owners also hung in the balance, were little angels!

Although we've had him for only a year, I can't imagine life without this spirited six-pound ball of fluff (we came to find out that he is a full-grown miniature Schnoodle.) The whole family is completely enamored of him. In addition to teaching the kids important lessons like responsibility and empathy, he taught me how to open my heart again after losing a beloved pet. Unconditional love and tiny paws – is there anything better?

—Jill at Gooseberry Patch

Animals are such
*agreeable friends*—
they ask no questions,
they pass no criticisms.

—*George Eliot*

*Treat the furry members of your family and don't forget Fido's friends too! Friends and neighbors will be touched if you remember their pet with a small gift of Good Dog Treats or Kitty Cookies.*

## Good Dog Treats

*Use a bone-shaped cookie cutter for these doggone good treats!*

3 c. all-purpose flour
3 c. whole-wheat flour
2 c. cracked wheat
1 c. cornmeal
2-1/2 t. garlic powder

1 T. brewers' yeast
1/2 c. powdered milk
3 c. beef broth, divided
2 T. milk

Combine dry ingredients in a large bowl. Stir in 2 cups broth to form a very stiff dough; gradually mix in remaining cup broth to form bread-dough consistency. On a floured surface, roll dough to 1/4-inch thickness. Use cookie cutters to cut dough into shapes; place biscuits on greased baking sheets. Lightly brush tops with milk. Bake at 300 degrees for 45 minutes; turn oven off without removing biscuits. Allow biscuits to sit overnight. Store in an airtight container. Makes 4-1/2 pounds.

# Kitty Cookies

*Cats will flip over these "cookies" made with real salmon!*

2 c. oil
2 c. cornmeal
¾ c. chicken broth

8-oz. can salmon, drained
2 c. whole-wheat flour

Combine all ingredients and mix well. Flatten out to 1/2-inch thick and cut with a cookie cutter. Bake on ungreased baking sheets at 325 degrees for 20 minutes; cool on a wire rack. Makes about 2 dozen.

For a "paws"-itively delightful presentation, copy this tag onto cardstock, cut out and attach to your bag of treats.

to:

from:

# Little Things Can Make a Big Difference

**A small gesture can make a big impact in the lives of those who are closest to us.**

A great way to get the kids involved... help an elderly neighbor rake leaves, shovel snow or weed flower beds.

Are you a part of a garden or craft club? Make floral arrangements for a senior center, nursing home or hospital. Cheery flowers brighten everyone's day!

A simple way to spread some cheer! Put out flags for the 4th of July in neighborhood front yards or the town center. In the spring, organize a neighborhood clean-up day, or plant flowers in common areas.

Are you an animal lover? Next time you're running errands, drop off a carload of newspapers, towels and blankets to an animal shelter.

Why not ask for donations of canned goods as the "price of admission" at your next get-together? Your local food pantry will thank you!

The next time your family goes to the movies, let the kids invite a friend. You'll brighten their day, and perhaps give another mom an unexpected treat...a free afternoon!

Have you told someone lately that you love them? Even better, make a list highlighting all of the different reasons you appreciate them. It's sure to become a treasured memento.

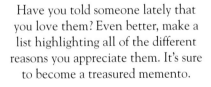

*Dear friends,
Just a note
to let you know
I'm thinking
of you...
~Yours
truly!*

Did you recently meet some folks who are new in town? Invite them to your next gathering...after all, the more, the merrier!

# Index

# Index

# Gooseberry Patch
*cookbooks*

Since 1992, we've been publishing our own country cookbooks for every kitchen and for every meal of the day! Each title has hundreds of budget-friendly recipes, using ingredients you already have on hand in your pantry.

In addition, you'll find helpful tips and ideas on every page, along with our hand-drawn artwork and plenty of personality. Their lay-flat binding makes them so easy to use...they're sure to become a fast favorite in your kitchen.

*Send us your favorite recipe*

and the memory that makes it special for you!* If we select your recipe for a brand-new **Gooseberry Patch** cookbook, your name will appear right along with it...and you'll receive a FREE copy of the book!

Submit your recipe on our website at

**www.gooseberrypatch.com**

or mail it to:

**Gooseberry Patch • Attn: Cookbook Dept.**
**2500 Farmers Dr., #110 • Columbus, OH 43235**

*Please include the number of servings and all other necessary information!